SCIENCE GETS PHYSICAL

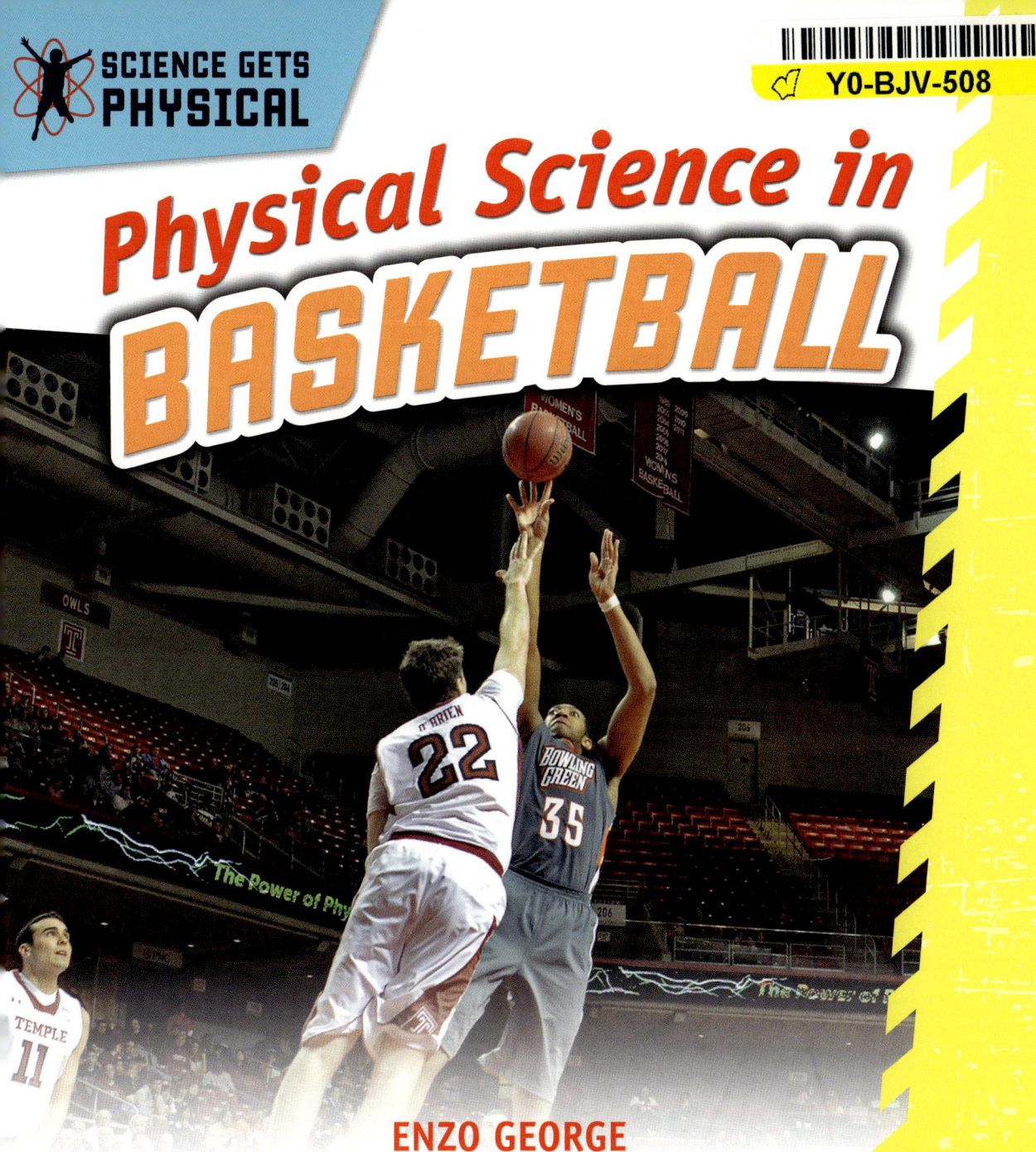

Physical Science in BASKETBALL

ENZO GEORGE

CRABTREE
PUBLISHING COMPANY
WWW.CRABTREEBOOKS.COM

Author: Enzo George
Editors: Sarah Eason, Jennifer Sanderson, and Elizabeth DiEmanuele
Consultant: David Hawksett
Editorial director: Kathy Middleton
Proofreader: Wendy Scavuzzo
Design: Paul Myerscough and Jeni Child
Design edits: Katherine Berti
Cover design: Lorraine Inglis
Photo research: Rachel Blount
Print and production coordinator: Katherine Berti

Written, developed, and produced by Calcium

Photo Credits:
t=Top, c=Center, b=Bottom, l= Left, r=Right

Inside: Inside: Flickr: Cliff: p. 29t; Shutterstock: ARENA Creative: p. 28–29; Aspen Photo: p. 1, 7, 8–9, 16–17, 26, 30–31, 34, 41; Fabrizio Andrea Bertani: p. 38; Goran Bogicevic: p. 6; Paolo Bona: p. 18; Brocreative: p. 5t; Anze Furlan: p. 40; Glenda: p. 14b; Icsnaps: p. 14–15t, 19; Alex Kravtsov: p. 12; Jacob Lund: p. 13; MaszaS: p. 32–33; Monkey Business Images: p. 10–11b; Sergey Novikov: p. 45; Eugene Onischenko: p. 27; Vasyl Shulga: p. 20–21; Sirtravelalot: p. 4–5b; Valentin Valkov: p. 31t; Ververidis Vasilis: p. 21t; Vectorpouch: p. 16b; Debby Wong: p. 39; Zhangjin_net: p. 11; U.S. Air Force: Johnny Wilson: p. 3, 24–25; Wikimedia Commons: Keith Allison, from Owings Mills, USA: p. 23c, 37b; Luis Blanco: p. 42; Adam Glanzman, Michigan Daily: p. 43; Kris Krüg from Vancouver, Canada: p. 35; New York World-Telegram and the Sun staff photographer: p. 33t; Fred Palumbo, World Telegram staff photographer: p. 9b; James Schumacher: p. 22–23b; Lorie Shaull: p. 36–37; Tim Shelby from Arlington, VA, USA: p. 25.

Cover: Shutterstock: Alex Kravtsov.

Library and Archives Canada Cataloguing in Publication

Title: Physical science in basketball / Enzo George.
Names: George, Enzo, author.
Description: Series statement: Science gets physical | Includes index.
Identifiers: Canadiana (print) 20190195398 | Canadiana (ebook) 20190195401 | ISBN 9780778775447 (hardcover) | ISBN 9780778775577 (softcover) | ISBN 9781427125194 (HTML)
Subjects: LCSH: Basketball—Juvenile literature.
Classification: LCC GV885.1 .G46 2020 | DDC j796.323—dc23

Library of Congress Cataloging-in-Publication Data

CIP available at the Library of Congress

LCCN: 2019043926

Crabtree Publishing Company
www.crabtreebooks.com   1-800-387-7650

Printed in the U.S.A./012020/CG20191115

Copyright © **2020 CRABTREE PUBLISHING COMPANY**. All rights reserved. No part of this publication may be reproduced, stored in a retrieval system or be transmitted in any form or by any means, electronic, mechanical, photocopying, recording, or otherwise, without the prior written permission of Crabtree Publishing Company. In Canada: We acknowledge the financial support of the Government of Canada through the Canada Book Fund for our publishing activities.

Published in Canada
Crabtree Publishing
616 Welland Ave.
St. Catharines, Ontario
L2M 5V6

Published in the United States
Crabtree Publishing
PMB 59051
350 Fifth Avenue, 59th Floor
New York, New York 10118

Published in the United Kingdom
Crabtree Publishing
Maritime House
Basin Road North, Hove
BN41 1WR

Published in Australia
Crabtree Publishing
Unit 3 - 5 Currumbin Court
Capalaba
QLD 4157

CONTENTS

CHAPTER 1   SCIENCE ON COURT   4
  Moving the Ball   6
  Anatomy of a Basketball Player   8

CHAPTER 2   HAVING A BALL   10
  Science That Bounces   12
  Forces on the Ball   14

CHAPTER 3   EQUIPMENT   16
  A Perfect Surface   18
  The Target   20
  Walking on Air   22

CHAPTER 4   JUMP!   24
  Anatomy of the Jump   26
  Hang Time   28

CHAPTER 5   SHOOTING HOOPS   30
  In a Spin   32
  Free Throw   34
  It's a Long Shot   36

CHAPTER 6   TRACKING PERFORMANCE   38
  Getting Technical   40
  March Madness   42

GET PHYSICAL!   44
GLOSSARY   46
LEARNING MORE   47
INDEX   48

CHAPTER 1
SCIENCE ON COURT

Basketball is one of the most exciting sports on Earth. Everything moves fast! Players pass the ball down the court, and **dribble** while running at full speed. Players leap so far toward the net that they seem to hang in the air. This fast-paced ball sport requires skill, strength, and **agility**. But did you know that there is also a lot of science involved?

In a basketball game, players not only face the other team, they also have to defy gravity.

Some of the Science

Anyone can shoot hoops in the gym, on an outdoor court, or even in their backyard. Even if you don't play in the National Basketball Association (NBA), you can learn a lot from the science of the game. For example, players who jump have to overcome **gravity**. They also need a great sense of balance to not fall over when they turn around.

Teams get 24 seconds to shoot when they take the ball. When the ball bounces on the ground, it is affected by a **force** called **friction**. The ball is also affected by other forces when it travels through the air.

The NBA uses **statistics**, such as the percentage of three-point shots, to measure how well a team plays. Some teams put these statistics into computer programs. They use what they learn to help coaches better prepare their teams for a game.

The Basics

In formal games, basketball is played by two teams of five players. A standard NBA court is 94 feet (28.7 m) by 50 feet (15.2 m). At both ends of the court is a basket: a hoop 18 inches (45.7 cm) in diameter positioned 10 feet (3 m) above the floor.

A basketball looks quite simple, but it is carefully designed to make it easier for players to hold, bounce, and throw.

The object of the game is to score points by passing the ball through the hoop.

A shot taken from outside the **arc**-shaped line scores three points. A shot taken from inside that line scores two points. Free throws, which are awarded when a player is **fouled**, are worth one point each.

Easy, right? Well, it is not as simple as it sounds. For scientists, basketball is one of the most complicated and most interesting sports.

Moving the Ball

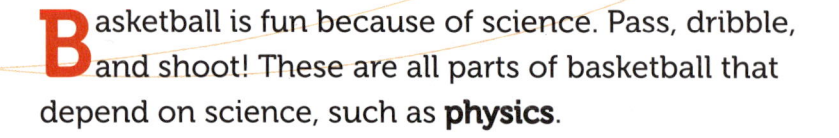

Basketball is fun because of science. Pass, dribble, and shoot! These are all parts of basketball that depend on science, such as **physics**.

End-to-End Play

Basketball is all about the ball. Good players can move the ball from one end of the court to the other in only a couple of seconds. The fastest way is just to throw the ball. A ball can travel through the air faster than a person can run. This is because the ball is smaller and lighter than a human body, so it is easier for it to move through the air. The smooth surface of the ball makes it easier for the air to pass around it. This reduces **air resistance**, or **drag**. When a player runs, their feet contact the ground. This contact creates friction, which slows the player down.

Basketball players bounce the ball to keep the other team from being able to grab it. This is called dribbling.

Dribble and Bounce

In official games, a player can only take two steps after catching the ball. If players take more steps, they get **penalized** for traveling. Players bounce the ball up and down on the floor. This skill is called dribbling.

Dribbling looks easy, but it is hard work. As soon as the ball hits the ground, physics slows it down. The player needs to push the ball down hard enough toward the floor to get it back under control.

GETTING PHYSICAL: ENERGY

In this photo, the player on the right is dribbling the ball. When you dribble a ball, you use two kinds of energy. When you hold the ball above the floor, it has **potential energy**. Potential energy is the energy an object has from its position and its ability to move. When you drop the ball, the potential energy changes to **kinetic energy**. Kinetic energy is movement energy. When the ball hits the floor, the kinetic energy makes it bounce back up.

The ball also loses some energy. Hitting with the ground causes friction, which takes some energy. It also creates energy in the form of heat and sound. The loss of energy means that a ball does not have enough kinetic energy to bounce back to its original height. To keep dribbling, you have to add extra energy by pushing it down toward the floor.

Anatomy of a Basketball Player

Everyone who plays basketball is an athlete. Taking a shot at the basket takes hand-eye coordination. Your brain has to figure out what angle to throw the ball. The more you practice, the better your brain remembers what angle to throw the ball and what force to use.

Getting Physical

Basketball players are always in motion. They can run and jump because of the system of muscles, **tendons**, and joints. Basketball players can also spin without falling because they have a strong sense of balance. Our sense of balance depends on what we can see with our eyes. Balance also depends on our ears.

When players jump to shoot or to block, they spring off the ground by straightening their hips, knees, and ankles at the same time.

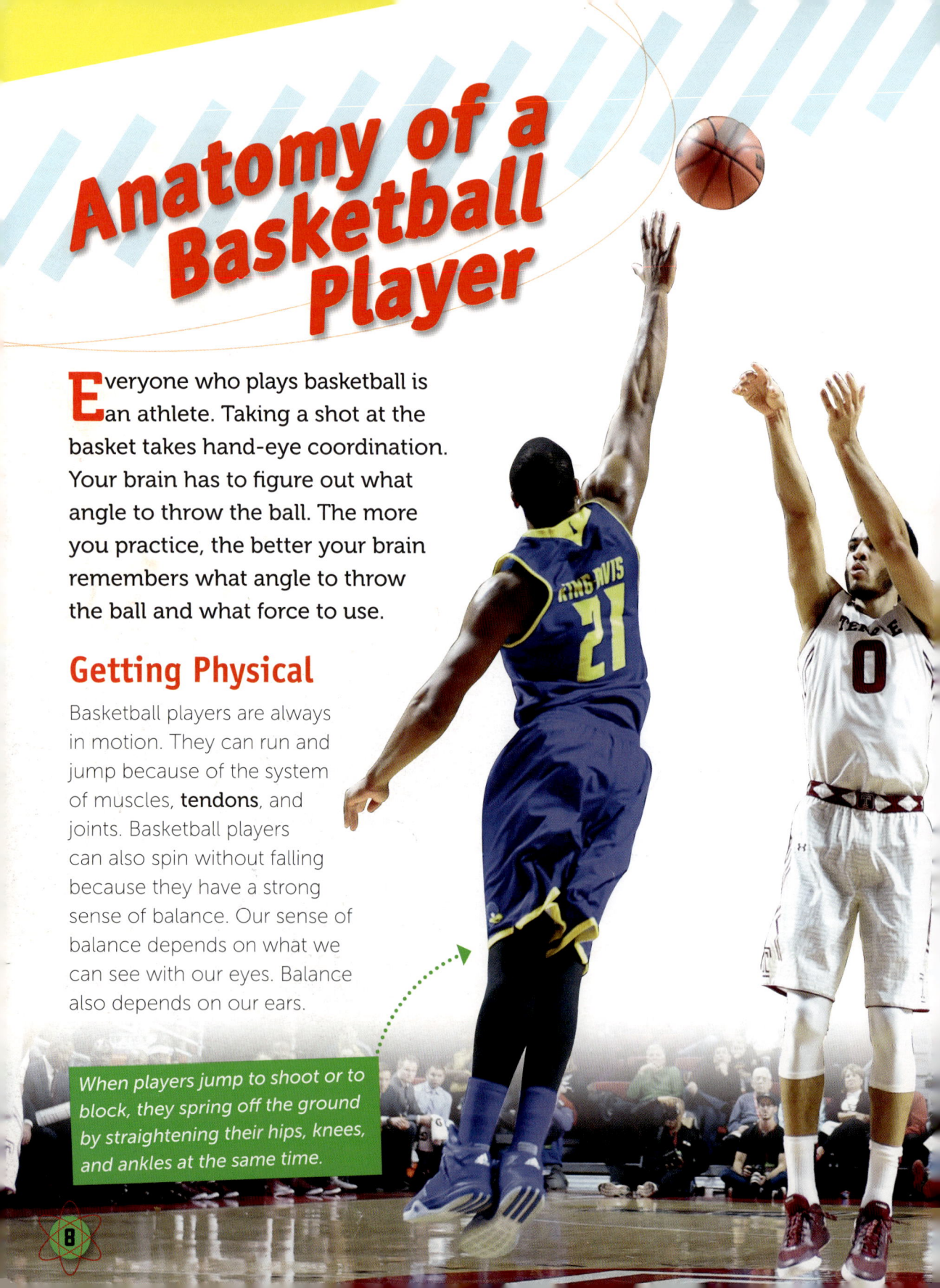

Inside each of our ears are three small semi-circular canals that hold a liquid. This is called the vestibular system. The liquid moves when our heads move, telling us where our bodies are in the space around them. This liquid helps keep everything in focus as we move around.

Tall and Lean

The rim of the basket is 10 feet (3 m) above the ground. This height means most of the action takes place up in the air. The taller players are and the longer their arms, the closer they can get to the basket. The lighter they are, the easier it is for them to overcome gravity and jump off the ground.

If you are not tall, do not worry. The shortest player to appear in the NBA was Muggsy Bogues. Muggsy played for the Charlotte Hornets and other teams. He was just 5 feet 3 inches (1.6 m) tall. Muggsy made himself tall when he needed to: he could jump 44 inches (111.7 cm) off the ground.

SCIENCE WINS!

WILT CHAMBERLAIN

In 1962, Wilt Chamberlain of the Philadelphia Warriors became the first player in the NBA to score 100 points in a game. The Warriors defeated the New York Knicks 169–147. Chamberlain's anatomy definitely helped. Nicknamed "Wilt the Stilt," he was 7 feet 1 inch (2.16 m) tall. With his arms above his head, he could reach 9.3 feet (2.8 m). Wilt also had larger hands. They were 9.5 inches (24 cm) long and 11.5 inches (29 cm) wide. Chamberlain's large hands helped him hold and control the ball with just one hand.

CHAPTER 2

HAVING A BALL

You can play basketball without a proper court. You can play with fewer or more than five players per team, or even on your own. You can even practice passing and dribbling without a hoop. But it is impossible to play basketball without the ball!

The perfect sphere of a basketball allows players to bounce, dribble, and slam the ball without breaking it.

Basketballs must be made from strong materials that can handle the pressure of the game.

The Science of Shape

There are different sizes of basketballs. For younger players, the ball can be 27 inches (68.6 cm) in **circumference**. For professional players, it can be up to 29.5 inches (74.9 cm). The ball gets filled up with air so that it is a regular **sphere**. The air and shape help it bounce. The first balls were made of leather stitched together around a rubber **bladder**. Today, most balls are a combination of **synthetic** materials, such as rubber.

These materials are molded into a perfect sphere using heat. They contain a rubber bladder. The bladder is wrapped in layers of materials, such as nylon and polyester. A basketball has to put up with a lot of wear and tear because it gets thrown and bounced. These inner materials help keep the ball round at all times.

What's Inside?

A basketball bounces because it contains pressurized air. Air is a mixture of gases, including oxygen, water vapor, and nitrogen. The **molecules**, or particles, in these gases are always moving. If they touch a surface, they push on it, creating pressure. A basketball is inflated with a pump. A pump pushes air inside the ball through a small valve, or opening.

When the air molecules get squeezed together, they push against the bladder of the ball. This keeps it inflated. A basketball has to be inflated to a pressure of about 8 pounds per square inch (psi) (55 kpa). The psi is a measure of how much pressure is applied to a specific area of the ball's inner surface. If a ball is inflated to fewer than 8 psi, it will not bounce well. If it is overinflated, it will stretch out of shape. The ball could even burst, just like how a balloon bursts if you blow too much air into it.

Science That Bounces

Bouncing a ball up and down the court is not as simple as you might think. In fact, just bouncing the ball involves a whole lot of physics.

Force is at work during basketball. This force is because of physics!

Why Do Balls Bounce?

There are three reasons the ball bounces: the air inside of the ball, gravity, and Newton's Laws of Motion. How do Newton's Laws of Motion work? When you dribble a basketball, your hand and gravity both push the ball toward the ground (Law 1). As it drops, the ball accelerates and speeds up (Law 2). The ball pushes into the ground when it hits it, **compressing** the air inside. The ground pushes up with an equal, but opposite amount of force. The force results in the ball bouncing back up into your hand (Law 3).

The energy in the compressed air moves back to the ball and pushes it back into motion. If you were to take your hand away and stop dribbling, the ball would continue to bounce. This would happen because of Newton's First Law. The ball would slow down and stop due to friction.

The more **air pressure** inside, the harder it will push on the sides of the ball and the more bounce you will get. This is why an underinflated ball will not bounce very well. The ball needs air pressure inside to keep the forces necessary for bounce.

GETTING PHYSICAL: FRICTION

Pebbling is the name for the bumps on the surface of the basketball. The bumps encourage friction. When objects hit each other, friction slows things down. This friction makes the ball easier for a player to use. They can grip, pass, and dribble without worrying about dropping the ball.

Forces on the Ball

Sometimes it seems as though the ball will not go where you aim it. In fact, the **trajectory**, or the path through the air, of any ball is always shaped by four forces.

Four Forces

There are four main forces that act on a basketball moving through the air. They are gravity, drag, the **Magnus force**, and **buoyancy**. Gravity is the force that pulls objects toward each other. Usually, gravity refers to the way Earth pulls everything to the ground. In the case of a basketball, gravity pulls the ball down.

GETTING PHYSICAL: FINGER SPIN

One of the most impressive basketball tricks is to spin the ball on the tip of your finger. This requires skill—and some help from science. The secret is in the spin. If you only place a ball on your fingertip, gravity will make it fall off. But, if you start it spinning horizontally by pushing it with your other hand, you create **momentum**. Momentum is the amount of motion that an object has, as a result of its **mass** (or weight) and **velocity** (or speed). An object's momentum stays the same until it is acted on by another force. The ball's momentum will keep it spinning until air resistance and the friction with your finger slow it down and it falls. As the ball is spinning, it creates centripetal force. This force pushes an object traveling in a circular path toward the center around which it is moving, so it keeps the ball from falling off your finger.

> The hoop is twice the diameter of the ball, so the ball should fit through easily. The target seems smaller because the ball is usually approaching it at an angle, not directly from above.

Drag is also known as air resistance. Molecules in the air oppose the progress of the ball as it moves through them, slowing it down. Gravity and drag explain why, if you throw a basketball in a straight line, it does not carry on forever. Soon, it loses energy, slows down, and falls to the ground.

The Magnus force causes the path of the ball to bend as it travels. This force happens because the ball spins as it travels. As the ball moves through the air, the spinning motion affects the air pressure. There is a slight difference in air pressure on opposite sides of the ball. One side has higher pressure than the other. The difference in air pressure pulls the ball toward the side with lower pressure. As a result, it creates a slight curve in the ball's path.

Buoyancy is a force that acts upward on the ball. This force is caused by a small difference in air pressure, which is lower at the top than at the bottom of the ball.

15

CHAPTER 3

EQUIPMENT

Imagine you are at a big basketball game. The gym is full. Everyone is excited. The game starts, but the players are soon falling over because the court is too slippery. On the first shot, the backboard breaks and the hoop falls on the floor. It is a disaster! Basketball equipment might seem simple, but it is all carefully designed.

The Court

The ball might be the most important piece of equipment, but official games must happen on a court. A full-size court is 94 feet (28.7 m) by 50 feet (15.2 m). It should be flat and have no **obstructions**.

For safety, there should be a clear area around the court. This area is for if players overshoot the sidelines and endlines. The areas of the court are marked out in lines that are 2 inches (5 cm) thick.

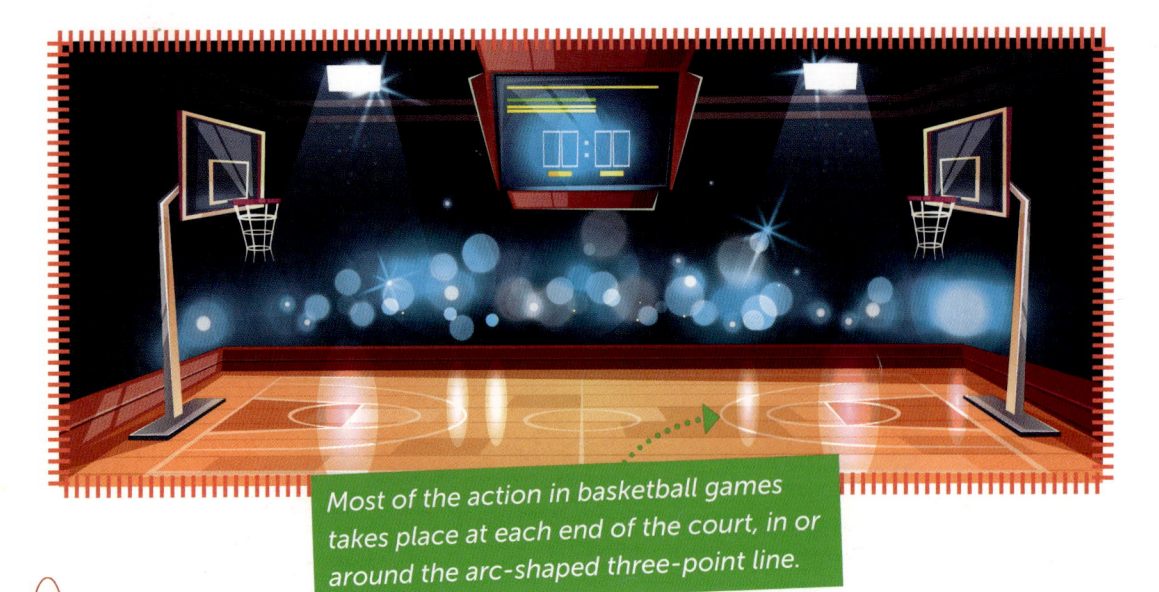

Most of the action in basketball games takes place at each end of the court, in or around the arc-shaped three-point line.

An indoor basketball court is usually made of wood or artificial materials. An outdoor court is usually made of concrete. These materials provide a good bounce for the ball. They are strong. They can handle the friction from shoes or the ball. They are also smooth, which keeps dirt from the ball from sticking to the court.

There are hoops at both ends of the court. The hoops are simple rings of metal. On a full-size court, these rings are 10 feet (3 m) above the ground. The hoops are attached to a backboard. The backboard is usually held up by a pillar or another frame that can move up or down for maintenance. Modern backboards are often see-through. This lets people sitting at the end of the court see the game. The backboards are made from special materials so that they do not shatter when hit by the ball. Attached to the hoop is a net, which slows the ball down when a basket is scored. The net also makes it easier to tell if a shot has passed through the hoop or missed it.

Uniforms

Basketball uniforms are designed to be as comfortable as possible for players. They are usually made of a blend of cotton and polyester. These materials are cool to wear and easy to wash. The uniform has tiny holes that allow heat to escape. The jerseys usually have no sleeves. The shorts have an elastic waistband to hold them up.

Long shorts are not needed for basketball. Modern players wear them because they look and feel great!

A Perfect Surface

If you have ever tried playing basketball on a grassy field, you know that it is almost impossible to make the ball bounce well. If you can even get it to bounce at all, it will not rise very high into the air. It could even go in a different direction. This happens because the grass and the soft earth absorb the energy of the ball. When the ball hits the grass, it does not have enough kinetic energy to spring back into the air. The blades of grass point in different directions, so the ball cannot bounce the same each time.

Hard Floors

A good surface for getting a basketball to bounce well is smooth hardwood. The amount of bounce depends on how hard the wood is. The hardest woods come from trees that grow slowly. These trees have cells that are packed closely together. Since the 1890s, the preferred wood has been maple. Maple has a very fine **grain** running through it. Maple is also easier to clean, because it has fewer cracks and spaces for dirt to gather. It also does not **splinter**, so it is easier on players if they fall. All NBA teams have maple courts except for the Boston Celtics, who have a red oak floor.

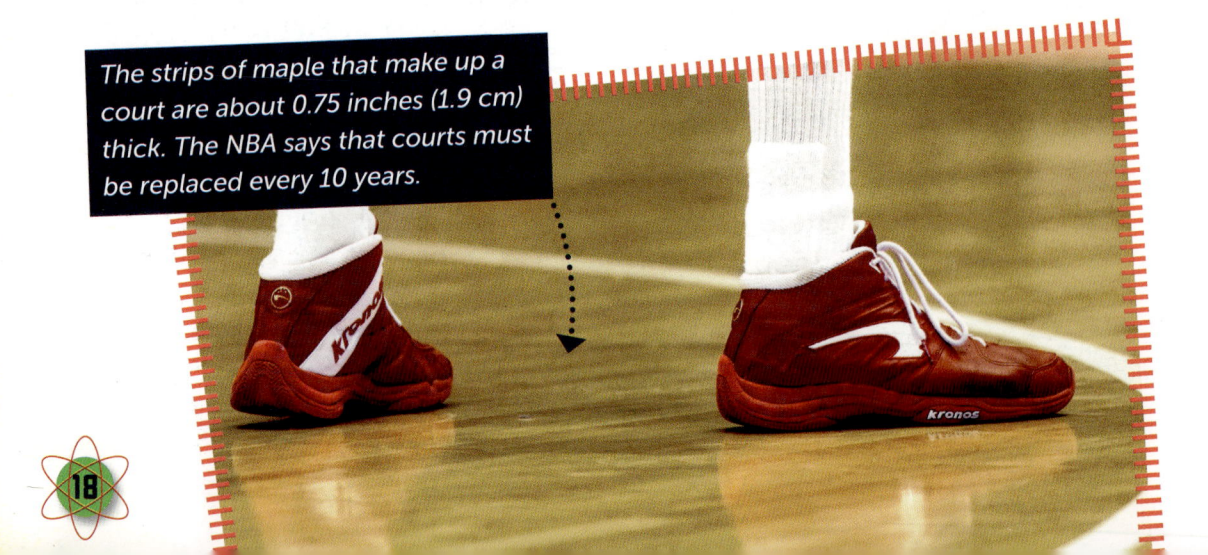

The strips of maple that make up a court are about 0.75 inches (1.9 cm) thick. The NBA says that courts must be replaced every 10 years.

Other Materials

Schools and other locations don't always use maple. Sometimes they are made from sections of plastic. The sections are placed on a concrete floor. Then they get put together like a giant puzzle. The plastic can be coated with a **polyurethane** layer to make it more **durable**.

Outdoors, the usual surface for a basketball court is concrete. This material is strong, but its uneven surface can cause cuts and scrapes if a player falls.

The surface of most outdoor courts is rough concrete or asphalt. The uneven surface provides increased friction that helps shoes grip the ground.

GETTING PHYSICAL: IMPACT

When you run, your feet hit the floor hard. The effect of your velocity adds force to the **impact**. The impact can be like up to five times your body weight is passing through the soles of your feet. Each time your foot lands, it absorbs a shock that passes up your legs. It can even compress your spine. Many basketball courts are designed to reduce impact on the players' legs. The court is supported above the concrete floor by a grid of ribs and empty spaces. This creates air cushioning. When the athlete's foot hits the court, some of the energy is absorbed downward through the floor, as well as upward into their leg. This reduces the shock of the impact.

The Target

The basketball hoop was originally a wooden peach basket. Today, it is a metal circle 1.5 feet (0.5 m) across and 10 feet (3 m) above the ground. Nothing could be simpler. Yet physics is at work even here. Beneath the rim hangs a tube-shaped net of cord. The cords of the net are woven, which gives it tension. The cords pull on one another and create more tension. Tension is a pulling force. When the ball drops through the net, this tension slows it down for a moment. The net makes it easier to see if a player scores a basket. Without a net, it can be difficult to tell if the ball passes through the hoop. The thin rim sometimes confuses the human eye.

The cord that hangs from the hoop is 15 to 18 inches (38 to 46 cm) long. It is knotted together to keep the mesh from becoming loose.

Seeing Clearly

The hoop is attached to a backboard that measures 3.5 feet (1 m) tall and 6 feet (1.8 m) wide. The backboard is marked with a square, also known as the target. The target is 18 inches (46 cm) high and 24 inches (61 cm) across. The backboard is there for the player. The player aims at the target so that a shot can bounce back from it and either fall into the net or rebound. When this does not happen, the ball goes out of play and the game stops.

Basketball Backboards

The first backboards were made of wood. But, in 1917, people sitting behind the basket complained, because they could not see the game. Since then, NBA backboards have been see-through. They are made of safety glass so that they do not break. Safety glass is made of specially treated glass that is much stronger than regular glass. If a player accidentally hits the backboard hard during a shot, the glass may crack into tiny square pieces, but they are not sharp. Some backboards are made from Plexiglas. This material is from a plastic called polymethyl methacrylate, or acrylic. It is clear and light, and it does not shatter.

GETTING PHYSICAL: SHOT CLOCK

Today, NBA games have a 24-second shot clock. Given that there are 60 seconds in a minute, this seems random! But it was carefully decided. The shot clock was introduced in 1954 to try to lead to higher-scoring games. The people who came up with it estimated that fans wanted to see about 120 shots in a game. That equals 48 minutes, or 2,880 seconds. Divided by 120, that gives 24 seconds per shot.

Walking on Air

One of the most important pieces of equipment for a basketball player is the right shoes. Basketball shoes need to give you a firm grip on a polished floor and help you stay balanced. They also need to fit your feet. You do not want your feet to slip inside your shoes when you make a jump at the basket.

Get a Grip!

The shoe soles are usually made of rubber or other synthetic materials. This provides traction for running and jumping. Traction is a form of friction. The sole of the shoe grips the surface of the court when the player's foot pushes against it. The traction then lets the player move without slipping. The rubber sole is often wider than the player's foot. The width adds stability. It also keeps the weight of the foot spread out inside the shoe. All of this helps the foot generate power and prevents injuries.

When a defender faces an attacker, both players need to be able to move in any direction without worrying about slipping.

There are 26 bones and 33 joints in the foot, and another 7 bones in the ankle. That means there is a lot that can go wrong if the foot is not kept flat inside a shoe.

The Uppers

Uppers are the part of the shoe that goes on top of the foot. In the past, uppers were made of canvas, leather, or suede. For example, the first basketball shoes, the famous Converse Chucks, were made with canvas uppers. Today, shoes are often made from synthetic mesh material. This material is lighter than leather and allows air in, keeping a player's feet cooler. In the past, uppers usually also had high tops around the ankle for extra support. The high tops stopped the ankle from twisting during a jump. Now, many shoes are missing this high top. Some experts blame an increase in foot and ankle injuries on this change.

Los Angeles Lakers guard Steve Blake pushes off the sole of one shoe as he passes the ball.

GETTING PHYSICAL: USING LAYERS

The sole of a basketball shoe is usually made in layers. This allows them to be made of more than one material. The rubber and other materials contain pockets of air. The pockets help cushion the impact of the feet on the court. The air pockets compress and absorb the shock of any impact before bouncing back into shape.

CHAPTER 4

JUMP!

There are few sports that need you to get off the ground more than basketball. The hoops are 10 feet (3 m) in the air, so being as high up in the air as possible makes it easier to score. Even for the tallest basketball players, that still means they need to be able to jump. They also have to run, turn, hurdle, throw, catch, and dribble.

Off the Ground

The average player in the NBA is 6 feet 7 inches (2.01 m) tall. That's very tall! The average American is 5 feet 9 inches (1.75 m). But, height alone cannot make a person good at basketball. In fact, many of the best players have been shorter than the average. What makes the best players is their ability to get height at the right times, such as when they are shooting, trying to catch a rebound, or leaping to block a shot or pass.

A well-timed jump can lift an attacker above a defender, giving a clear shot at the basket.

There are many kinds of jumps in basketball. Players jump with a run-up or as they spin, or they can jump from a standing start. They jump forward, twist in the air, or just jump straight up into the air. They jump off one foot or off both feet. There are two main types of jumps. First, the standing jump, when the athlete makes the jump from a **stationary** position. Second, the hurdle jump, when someone runs, then leaps into the air off one foot.

Vertical Jumps

One way to measure how high people can jump is a **vertical** jump test. In this, the player stands still. Then, they use their body to spring straight up into the air, as high as possible. This jump measures how high the player's feet rise above the ground. The average vertical jump for players in the NBA is 28 to 30 inches (71 to 76 cm). Some players can reach more than 40 inches (101 cm) high.

The vertical jump test is a good measure of a player's ability to create force in a jump. But there are a few times in a basketball game when a player makes a **static** jump straight up into the air.

Modern tests combine jumping with speed and agility tests. They combine these tests to find out who can generate the most power the fastest. Once a player is off the ground, they go up at the same speed. The advantage comes when a player can take off quicker or with more momentum.

LeBron James of the Los Angeles Lakers has one of the highest leaps in the NBA. He has a vertical jump of nearly 40 inches (102 cm).

Anatomy of the Jump

The height a basketball player can jump off the ground comes down to training and physics. Height comes from the power of your muscles in relation to your weight. Your weight is the load you have to lift off the ground.

Max Power!

The power behind a jump depends on two factors: strength and velocity. Strength, or force, is the greatest output of your muscles. Velocity is the greatest amount of speed you have. Players can learn to jump higher. They can do so by increasing their strength or velocity in relation to their body weight. It is much easier to jump off the ground while you are running than while you are standing still. Velocity multiplies the amount of force your muscles supply to produce more power. There is an equation to remember this: power = force x velocity.

GETTING PHYSICAL: THE SLAM DUNK

Nothing gets basketball fans on their feet like a slam dunk. A player leaps toward the net at high speed with the ball in their hands. As the player reaches the net, they slam down the ball through the hoop. The forward velocity of the run helps the player take off. They travel fast through the air because of the lack of friction. The player's outstretched arms act as a **lever** rotating around a **fulcrum** formed by the shoulder. This lever increases the force of the slam dunk.

To make a jump, the muscles **contract** very quickly around joints in the feet, ankles, knees, and hips. This contraction causes torque, or rotation, in the joints, which straighten up to achieve lift. It is the lift that raises us off the ground. Our bodies are quite heavy. It takes a lot of force to overcome gravity and leave the ground. The muscles will produce more power if they are more like a spring. Players need to train to keep their muscles as **flexible** as possible.

Biomechanics

Another influence on a player's jump is **biomechanics**. Biomechanics is the way the whole body comes together to make a jump as high as possible. If you swing your arms up powerfully as you jump, that lifts some of your body mass off your legs. Your legs then have a lighter load to lift into the air, so you can jump a little higher.

> Tucking your legs beneath you helps reduce drag from air resistance, helping you travel farther through the air.

Hang Time

When the greatest players leap toward the basket for a slam dunk, they seem to break the laws of physics. It is as though they break free of gravity and hang in the air for as long as they need to dunk the ball. This is called hang time. It is a physical achievement, but it is also an **optical illusion**.

Trapped by Gravity

Gravity is all over the world. The force of gravity is 32 feet per second squared (9.8 m/second squared). This measurement is the acceleration (or increase in velocity) with which gravity pulls everything back to Earth. From a running jump, the average person can stay in the air for about 0.53 seconds. No one can stay in the air for longer than 1 second. Michael Jordan's longest hang time is 0.92 seconds. That is almost double what an ordinary person can do. Michael Jordan's speed and force give him the power to launch himself off the ground. In the air, he has time to use biomechanics, moving his arms and legs, to help "kick" himself forward.

A running jumper follows a flight path that is curved like a semicircle. The player rises to the highest point off the ground, before getting pulled back to the ground in a curve. Most of the time that they are in the air is in the top half of the jump.

A running jump will help anyone jump higher than a standing jump. The player's speed multiplies the force of their leap.

SCIENCE WINS!

MICHAEL JORDAN

Michael Jordan (in the photo above) is seen as one of the greatest basketball players of all time. He is known as "Air Jordan." His nickname comes from his ability to take off from the free-throw line and fly 15 feet (4.6 m) to score slam dunks. While playing, Jordan was famous for his hang time. This hang time was partly an illusion created by his speed and the height of his jump. Jordan's ability to kick and straighten his body while he was in the air made it seem as if he was taking a second "jump." This was also simply another optical illusion.

SHOOTING HOOPS

A basketball hoop is twice as wide as a standard basketball. But, this does not mean it is easier to score a basket. Most of the time, the ball approaches the hoop at an angle. The angle reduces the surface area of the top of the basket, which makes scoring more difficult. The player must be accurate and also use angles.

The Right Angle

In a dunk, the player lets go of the ball above the hoop. Every other type of shot begins below that level. The ball travels in a curved path called an arc. When the ball reaches the top of the curve, it begins to fall because gravity and air resistance slow it down. The trick is figuring out the right curve. At the correct angle, the ball goes across the rim of the hoop and drops into the basket.

It is easy to get the angle of a shot wrong. When that happens, instead of landing in the net, the ball rebounds off the backboard or the rim. That is why catching rebounds is a vital skill.

Most of the time, players who shoot cannot see the circle of the hoop at all. In this case, all they see is the horizontal metal rim.

Sports and Warfare

As a basketball passes through the air, forces affect a few things. Force decides how far the basketball travels, the path it travels, and when it falls to the ground. This is called ballistics. This is the area of physics that looks at how objects act in flight. Ballistics links basketball to war. The science began when gunners had to figure out how to hit a target by firing heavy balls from a cannon. They had to set the angle of the cannon. The angle helped the ball go up into the air in a straight line. Then, the ball reached the top of its curve and was pulled by gravity onto the target. Gunners became experts at using math to figure out angles.

Basketball players are also experts at angles. Players learn through practice how hard they need to shoot the ball to score. All their shots can be studied using math. The perfect angle for a shot depends on how hard the ball is thrown and how far the shooter is from the basket. Angles can range. For shots from beyond the three-point line, the angle is about 45 degrees. For shots where the player stands 2 feet (60 cm) from the net, the angle is about 72 degrees.

In a Spin

Most times a basketball is passed or shot, it seems to fly straight through the air. In fact, it is almost always spinning around its own **axis** as it flies. This changes the ball's path. The spin is why the ball sometimes bends in the air. It is also why the best players always seem to be able to drop the ball off the backboard into the hoop.

Magnus Force

As air passes over the ball's spinning surface, the air pressure is greater on one side than on the other. This creates the Magnus force. The Magnus force causes the ball to bend as it flies. This force can curve balls in all sorts of sports, such as golf, tennis, soccer, and baseball.

The closer you are to the hoop, the more you need to throw the ball close to straight up in the air, so it drops on target.

Types of Spin

There are three main types of spin: topspin, sidespin, and backspin. In topspin, the ball spins vertically in the direction it travels. When a ball with topspin hits the ground, it seems to bounce forward with a kick. This bounce happens because the spin gives it greater speed. In sidespin, the ball spins horizontally as it travels. This spin increases the chances of its path bending one way or the other. In backspin, the ball spins vertically against the direction it travels. This slows the ball down when it hits any still surface, such as the floor, the backboard, or the rim.

Basketball players use their hands and wrists to put spin on the ball when they pass, throw, or shoot. The pebbling on the surface of the ball helps. The sunken ribs that divide the ball into panels also help. (There are usually eight panels, but sometimes ten.) These ribs allow the player to get enough grip on the ball's surface to start it spinning.

Backspin

If you want to score baskets, the spin to learn is backspin. Backspin helps slow down a shot when it hits the backboard or rim. It also slightly changes the angle of the ball's rebound. From there, the ball hits the board and goes down into the basket. But you still have to be on target to score!

SCIENCE WINS!

KAREEM ABDUL-JABBAR

In the 1970s and 1980s, Kareem Abdul-Jabbar (photo above) scored 15,837 field goals. That's more goals than anyone else at the time. His trademark shot was the skyhook. With the skyhook, he turned side-on to the basket as he jumped with the ball in one hand. At the top of his jump, he hooked his arm up and over. Then, he released the ball at the highest point with a flick of the wrist that applied backspin. Abdul-Jabbar used the hook shot farther from the basket than most players. With these shots, the ball followed a higher arc than others. That earned his shot the nickname "skyhook."

Free Throw

Keri Pryor of the Duquesne University Dukes goes into the zone as she prepares to take a free throw. In a situation like this, success depends as much on mental strength as it does on physical strength.

The clock is ticking down. The scores are tight. Crunch time. You break toward the net, and you draw a foul. Free throw! You stand on the line with the ball. It is just you and the basket. If you get it right, victory is yours!

A Constant Challenge

The free throw is the only shot in basketball that is constant. It is always taken from the same place on the court. The shooter is always free from defenders. There are only three **variables**, assuming the player always aims correctly. These are the height the player's hands are above the floor during the shot, the speed of the shot, and the spin of the ball. Top players practice hundreds of free throws. They practice until their muscles can remember everything. For example, the right speed to throw the ball and the best angle, so that they make the basket.

Dwyane Wade shoots a free throw for Team USA against China in the 2008 Olympics. Through his career, he scored nearly seven of every ten free throws that he took.

Free throws often get studied by a computer. Players use the information to figure out how to improve.

Do the Math

In terms of math, the player should release the ball about 7 feet (2.1 m) above the ground. They should apply enough backspin so that the ball spins about three times. The shot should be an angle of about 51 degrees. This angle will take the ball in an arc in which the highest point is virtually level with the top of the backboard. An arc also helps the ball reach the rim of the basket slowly. That means that if the ball hits the rim or the backboard, there is less chance of it rebounding. Experts believe there is more chance of success if a player aims for the back of the basket, instead of the front.

GETTING PHYSICAL: HOLDING YOUR NERVE

The math of free throws is simple. But no one thinks about math when they are standing on the free-throw line. Sometimes late in games, players tend to "choke." This means they forget their training and do not perform as well as usual. Some coaches are trying new methods of practice to overcome this problem. Instead of asking players to shoot hundreds of free throws in training, they use many types of unusual or unexpected training drills. The idea is to make the players' brains more adaptable. Even at home, anyone taking a free throw needs to relax and shoot!

It's a Long Shot

During half-time, you might have seen fans throw the ball the length of the court. In real games, these shots are rare. They need strength, accuracy, and luck. But, shooting from outside the arc is vital. Most points scored are three-pointers.

Cecilia Zandalasini jumps to take a three-point shot. The ball's arc means it can travel above the defender's hand and still fall back into the net.

A Dramatic Change

The three-point shot came to the NBA in 1979. Before that, most points were two-point field goals. The new rules changed the game dramatically. In 1979, three-pointers were only 3 percent of teams' attempted shots. By 2016, they made up more than 28 percent of all shots. Players realized they could score big without having to get through the players near the net. They began practicing taking longer shots from all over the opponent's half of the court.

Practice is important. Practice trains a player's muscles to throw the ball with enough strength to make sure it reaches the net. Players can add more power to the ball if they jump as they shoot. In a jump shot, the energy the player uses to take off from the floor is also **transmitted** to the ball.

From Every Angle

Players also have to practice angles. Physicists say that the ball should leave the player's hand at an angle of at least 33 degrees to score. The angle creates an arc. The arc gives the ball a chance of dropping into the basket. The speed the ball gets released is also important, because it affects how fast it moves and how far it will travel. The ball needs to travel fast enough so it does not fall short, but not so fast that it rebounds.

SCIENCE WINS!

BARON'S MAGIC SHOT

The success rate of three-pointers is quite high. Ray Allen (right photo) scored more three-point shots than anyone in NBA history. Ray's success rate was about 40 percent. But, beyond the half court, shooting success drops a lot. The success rate falls to about 1 percent. Players usually attempt these shots only when time is running out at the end of a quarter. In 2001, Baron Davis was playing for the Charlotte Hornets against the Milwaukee Bucks. With only 0.7 seconds left in the third quarter, Davis got the ball near his own endline. He threw a huge one-handed shot high into the air. This was the NBA's longest-ever basket, at 89 feet (27 m).

CHAPTER 6

TRACKING PERFORMANCE

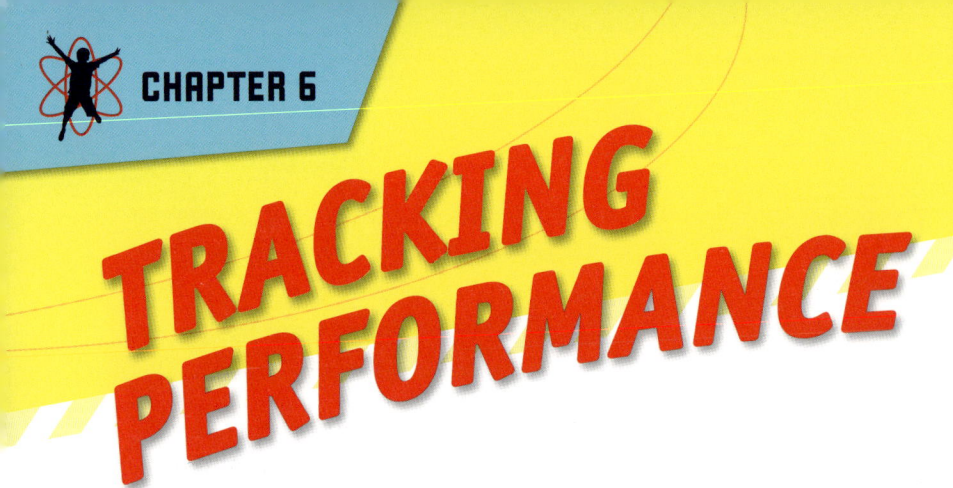

The NBA is often used for sports analysis. This is because of its small area and low team numbers.

Stat Attack

During a game, a basketball court seems full of action. Players are in motion, the ball is bouncing around, and arms and legs seem to be going everywhere. No two plays are exactly the same. Every moment is different. It all looks quite random but, in fact, basketball can be analyzed in an accurate, statistical way. Statistics make it possible to find patterns in the randomness of the game.

There have always been basketball statistics, such as how well a player shoots. To find this out, statistics record the number of shots a player takes. Then, it records the number of baskets scored. The result is a percentage. This percentage guesses the number of baskets a player would score from 100 shots.

Plays are carefully planned. Every player must understand their role in the team to create a shot opportunity.

Modern Statistics

Modern basketball uses new kinds of statistics. These are not always clear to the live audience. For example, it is easy to use cameras to track the path of the ball and the motion of the players. Teams use computer science to try to improve.

There are many computer programs that study the position of the ball. They also study the players. The programs turn this information into statistics, such as the speed teams move up the court. Coaches use this information to improve their teams.

It has also led to a whole new area of interest for basketball fans. Many sport fans love to discuss statistics. They use statistics to decide who was the best player in a position. In the past, these conversations did not have a lot of evidence. But, it is now possible to have all the statistics available.

A close game can be hard to watch. Luckily, modern technology makes score decisions more accurate.

Getting Technical

Coaches try to find any little way that will help them get ahead. Since 2010, teams have had cameras above and around the court. The cameras track the movement of players and the ball. They use computers to analyze all the information they gather.

Computer Checking

Computer programs then set out to analyze what teams did well and what they did not do well. They see where plays broke down and where the opposition players were at the time. They check which players did the best. They can also check on the performance of players, such as how far or fast they run or how many times they bounce the ball.

Coaches use video of training drills to learn where players need to improve.

Modern Analysis

In the past, coaches studied games by watching videos. That took a lot of time. Computers are much faster. They study hundreds of games. They can also study thousands or even millions of individual passes and shots. Now, coaches can spend more time helping their players.

Artificial intelligence (AI) plays an important part. In AI, machines can be programmed to "think" in the same kind of way a person does. Computers receive so much data that they can learn patterns, such as what defensive plays work best against a particular team. This is known as deep learning.

GETTING PHYSICAL: YOU'RE HIRED!

When they try to find a new player, coaches usually study videos and statistics. They call in the player for tests, such as making them throw hundreds of shots and free throws. Deep-learning systems have made this simpler, quicker, and more reliable. They can study millions of shots. Coaches can also film a player making a few dozen shots. Then, they put the data into a computer. The computer can then figure out how accurate the player is likely to be.

March Madness

Every spring, the top 68 teams in college basketball play. The tournament is the National Collegiate Athletics Association (NCAA). The teams play a series of knockout games, known as March Madness. They play until there are two teams left. The final two teams play the final. This game decides who becomes the national champions.

Reaching the Tournament

There are more than 352 schools in the division. That means that even getting to the last 68 teams takes a lot of skill. It also takes math, statistics, and probability, which is predicting how likely certain events are to happen.

There is also a selection committee. This committee is made up of 10 basketball administrators from the whole NCAA Division I. The committee studies each team.

For players such as Nolan Smith, who played for Duke University, the NCAA is a pathway into professional basketball in the NBA.

They think about the level of the opposition, and if games were played at home or away. They also find out the team's NCAA Evaluation Tool (NET) ranking. NET tries to measure not just wins and losses, but also how well they play. Once the committee has made its decisions, it also ranks the 68 teams. This means it ranks them in order of their apparent skill. Four teams are knocked out early in regional tournaments. This happens before the remaining 64 are put into the main tournament bracket. A bracket has a list of 16 pairs of teams on both sides. These are the first round of games.

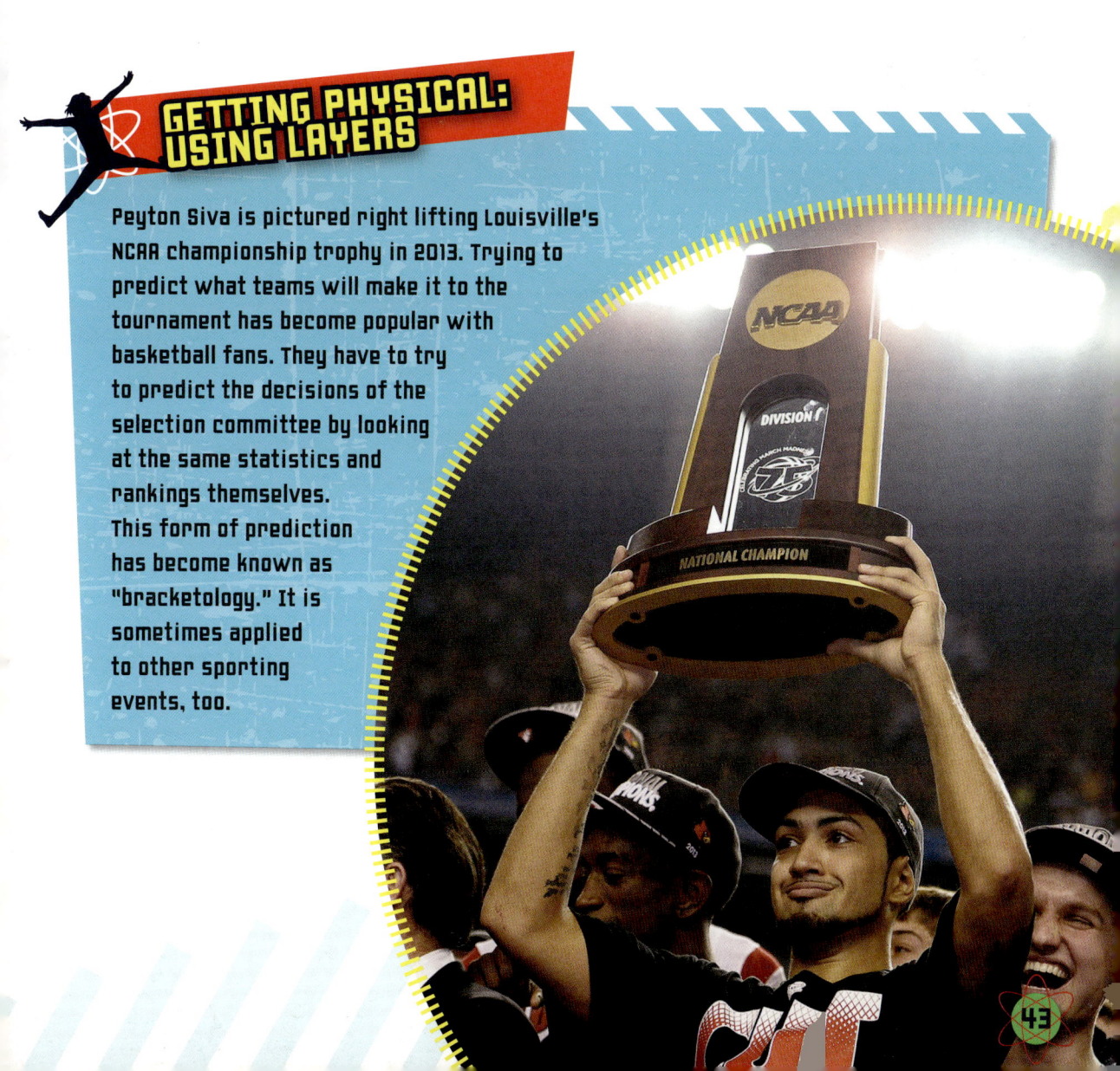

GETTING PHYSICAL: USING LAYERS

Peyton Siva is pictured right lifting Louisville's NCAA championship trophy in 2013. Trying to predict what teams will make it to the tournament has become popular with basketball fans. They have to try to predict the decisions of the selection committee by looking at the same statistics and rankings themselves. This form of prediction has become known as "bracketology." It is sometimes applied to other sporting events, too.

GET PHYSICAL!

It is time to find out for yourself something about the science of basketball. In this experiment, you will learn about how a ball bounces on different surfaces. You will also learn what forces might be responsible for this. The experiment needs at least two people. Find a friend or friends to help you.

YOU WILL NEED:
- Basketball
- Tape measure or ruler
- Masking tape
- Video camera or phone camera for filming
- Different surfaces to test, such as a basketball court, a carpet, grass, and concrete. These must be near a wall.

Instructions

1. Choose your first surface. You will test each surface separately.

2. Use the masking tape and tape measure or ruler to mark 8-inch (20 cm) gaps on the wall. Do this from where the wall meets the floor to a height of 40 inches (102 cm). You should end up with five horizontal strips of tape. This tape will help you measure the bounce of the ball.

3. Make sure the camera is set up so it can film all the strips of tape.

4. Hold the ball so that the bottom is level with the top strip of tape.

5. Drop the ball and film it. Do not push the ball down.

6. Drop and film the ball two or three more times.

7. Repeat the same experiment on more surfaces. Make sure that at least one surface is hard and one is soft.

8. Watch the bounces on video. For each surface, record how high the ball bounces by using the strips of tape.

9. Figure out the average bounce for each surface.

Analysis

Did the ball bounce higher on a hard or soft surface? Why do you think that happened?

Conclusion

When you hold the ball above the ground, it has potential energy. When you drop it, that energy becomes kinetic energy. When the ball hits the ground, some of that kinetic energy turns into heat. Some is also absorbed by the floor itself. That leaves less kinetic energy to push the ball back into the air. The height the ball bounces depends on the surface. You probably found that the ball bounced higher from hard surfaces. A harder surface absorbs less kinetic energy. This leaves more energy in the ball. A softer surface, such as grass, absorbs more kinetic energy. This means the ball bounces lower.

One surface you could test is asphalt or tarmac. You can find this on outdoor basketball courts or tennis courts.

45

GLOSSARY

agility The ability to move quickly and easily

air pressure The force exerted onto a surface by the weight of air

air resistance A force that acts in the opposite direction of an object traveling through air, slowing it down

anatomy The structure and workings of the body

arc A smooth curve

axis An imaginary line around which an object rotates

biomechanics The study of the physical laws relating to the movement of living things

bladder An inflated, hollow bag

buoyancy A force that acts upward on the ball

circumference The distance around the rim of a circle or sphere

compressing Squeezing

contract To shorten

drag When molecules slow something down

dribble To bounce the ball up and down on the floor

durable Long-lasting

flexible Able to bend easily without breaking

force An interaction that changes the motion of something

fouled Broke the rules against a player

friction The resistance created when one surface moves over another

fulcrum The point where a lever is placed to turn

grain The texture in a piece of wood

gravity A force that attracts things toward the center of Earth, or toward any other physical body

impact The action of one object hitting another

kinetic energy The energy an object has because of its motion

lever A bar that rests on a fulcrum and is used to move a load

Magnus force The effect that causes the ball to bend as it travels

mass The quantity of matter in an object (its "weight")

molecules Particles formed by atoms coming together

momentum The amount of motion of a moving body, measured as a product of its mass and velocity

obstructions Things that get in the way of movement

optical illusion Something that appears to be different from what it actually is

penalized Punished

physics The branch of science that studies materials and energy

polyurethane A strong humanmade rubber

potential energy The energy possessed by an object because of its mass and position

sphere A round, three-dimensional object

splinter A sharp chip or spike of wood

static Not moving, or jumping from a stationary position

stationary Not moving

statistics The science of collecting and studying information in the form of numbers

synthetic Artificial

tendons Flexible cords that attach muscles to bones

trajectory The path followed by a flying object, such as a ball

transmitted Passed from one thing to another

variables Features that can change

velocity Speed in a specific direction

vertical Upright, at right angles to the ground

LEARNING MORE

Find out more about the physics of basketball.

Books

Bethea, Nikole Brooks. *The Science of Basketball* (The Science of Sports with Max Axiom). Capstone Press, 2015.

Gardner, Robert and Dennis Shortelle. *Slam Dunk! Science Projects with Basketball* (Score! Sports Science Projects). Enslow Publishers, 2009.

Kalman, Bobbie, and John Crossingham. *Slam Dunk Basketball* (Sports Starters). Crabtree Publishing, 2007.

Stuckey, Rachel. *Full Court Press: Basketball Skills and Drills* (Basketball Source). Crabtree Publishing, 2016.

Websites

For a fun science project, log on at:
https://basketballstem.weebly.com/index.html

For a fun look at the forces behind backspin and more, visit:
www.labroots.com/trending/infographics/2931/science-basketball

This website looks at the science behind basketball:
www.sciencebuddies.org/blog/basketball-science-on-the-court

INDEX

Abdul-Jabbar, Kareem 33
air pressure 13, 15, 32
air resistance 7, 14, 15, 27, 31
Allen, Ray 37
analysis of performance 38–41, 43
anatomy 8–9
artificial intelligence (AI) 41

backboards 17, 20–21
ball design 10–11, 13, 32
ball flight 14–15, 31, 32–37
biomechanics 27, 28
Blake, Steve 23
Bogues, Muggsy 9
bouncing 5, 7, 10, 11, 12–13, 17, 18, 20, 31, 32, 38, 40, 44–45
bracketology 43

centripetal force 14
Chamberlain, Wilt 9
courts 16–17, 18–19

Davis, Baron 37

field goals 33, 36
finger spins 14

free throws 34–35
friction 5, 7, 13, 14, 17, 19, 22, 26
fulcrums 26

gravity 4, 9, 13, 14, 15, 27, 28–29, 31

hang time 28–29
height of players 9, 24
hook shots 33
hoop design 5, 9, 17, 20

impacts 19, 23

James, LeBron 4, 25, 28
Jordan, Michael 28, 29
jumping 24–29, 33, 36

kinetic energy 7, 18, 45

laws of motion 13
levers 26
long shots 36–37

Magnus force 14, 15, 32
March Madness 42–43
momentum 14, 25

National Basketball Association (NBA) 4, 5, 9, 10, 18, 21, 24, 25, 37, 38, 42

National Collegiate Athletics Association (NCAA) 42–43
Newton's Laws of Motion 13

potential energy 7, 45
probability 42
Pryor, Keri 34

rebounds 5, 20, 24, 31, 33, 35, 37, 38

shoes 22–23
shooting hoops 30–37
shot clocks 21
Siva, Peyton 43
slam dunks 26, 28, 29, 36
Smith, Nolan 42
spin 14, 15, 32–33, 34, 35, 37, 41
statistics 5, 36, 38–39, 41, 42, 43

three-point shots 5, 16, 31, 36–37
traction 22

uniforms 17

Wade, Dwyane 35

Zandalasini, Cecilia 36